THE BEST OF House Plants

Susanne Mitchell B.Sc.(Hort.)

Hamlyn
London · New York · Sydney · Toronto

ACKNOWLEDGEMENTS

We should like to thank the following for providing the
colour and black and white photographs used in this book:

Amateur Gardening
Pat Brindley, Robert Corbin,
John Cowley, Ernest Crowson,
Ken Muir, Thomas Rochford and Sons Ltd.,
and the
Harry Smith Horticultural Photographic Collection.

First Published in 1975 by
The Hamlyn Publishing Group Limited
London · New York · Sydney · Toronto
Astronaut House, Feltham, Middlesex, England

Second impression, 1976

Printed in Hong Kong by
Leefung-Asco Printers Limited

Filmset in England by
Tradespools Limited, Frome, Somerset
Set in 10 on 11 pt Monophoto Baskerville

ISBN 0 600 31368 9

Contents

Choosing Plants for the Home

Choosing plants for different situations in the home can be as much fun, and is as important, as selecting any other furnishing accessory. Every room is improved by the addition of one of the many lovely plants available for this purpose and most styles of modern furniture and architecture need the complementary presence of a house plant to be seen at their best.

Strictly speaking there is no such thing as a house plant. This is merely a collective term used to describe a number of exotic plants, from regions warmer than our own, which will adapt fairly readily to being grown indoors provided an attempt is made to meet their requirements. I do not want, however, to imply that there need be any mystic or ritual to accompany the successful growing of plants indoors. The secret of having 'green fingers' lies in giving plants the growing conditions they need, or, much easier, growing only those plants suited to the degree of temperature, light and humidity available. I suppose ideal conditions might be described as a draught-free room with good light, an equable temperature and high humidity. How few of us can hope to achieve that! But if you live in a house without central heating, or where the temperature fluctuates throughout the day, then select plants which can cope with this. There will be little hope of growing an anthurium or croton well in such conditions but an aspidistra, ivy, fatsia or rhoicissus will exist quite happily.

Temperature and humidity

When assessing your room conditions take into account first the degree of heat available and whether this is constant or fluctuates throughout the day. Plants should be positioned away from any hot spots which are found close to sources of heat as these cause an increase in temperature in the immediate surroundings.

Humidity is moisture which has evaporated into the air, and its main purpose as far as plants are concerned is to keep them from drying out too rapidly through loss of moisture from their leaves. High humidity is air which contains a lot of moisture and low humidity is air which is low in moisture. In average rooms the air tends to be low in moisture and becomes progressively so as the temperature rises. But many of the most popular house plants come from warm, moist regions, and to grow these successfully some way of increasing the humidity must be found (see page 17).

The plants in the trough – peperomia, anthurium and ivy – are plunged in moss to increase the humidity. *Dracaena marginata* is behind the chair and *Begonia masoniana* on the small table.

Good plants for average conditions: *Ficus elastica schryvereana* (left back) with *Neoregelia carolinae tricolor* in front, *Cissus antarctica* (right back) and *Tradescantia tricolor*

Above
A group arrangement of *Pteris cretica,* azalea, *Begonia* rex and *Maranta leuconeura kerchoreana*

Right
This profusion of good foliage plants for average home conditions includes *Maranta leuconeura kerchoveana, Chlorophytum comosum variegatum, Begonia rex, Pilea* Moon Valley and *Peperomia caperata tricolor*

A decorative grouping of *Ficus elastica* (left background) with *Neoregelia carolinae tricolor* in front, and *Calathea ornata sanderiana* (right background) with *Hedera helix* Glacier in front

Light and air

Plants differ widely in the amount of light they need but few foliage plants can withstand direct sunshine for any length of time as the sun's rays concentrated through the glass can burn the foliage. Artificial light has no harmful effect on plants; on the contrary it can give a useful boost to the level of light available.

The provision of sufficient air is essential to keep plants growing well with the minimum of disease but nothing is more detrimental than standing them in a draught, so a position in line with the door and windows may be unacceptable. A window-sill is an obvious choice of posi-

tion for plants, so much so that plant windows with specially constructed sills are now being incorporated into modern house design. This is ideal for supplying the level of light but beware of strong sunshine. Curtains may present another pitfall as so often they cut down the light transmitted or form a shield to the plants on the window-sill from the warmth of the room when drawn on cold winter evenings. In such cases it is better to move the plants into the room in the evenings or protect them by placing a thick layer of newspaper between them and the glass. Plants growing on window-sills should be turned frequently to encourage them to grow evenly.

Plants for various situations

For a sunless room: *minimum temperature 16°C. (60°F.)* Aglaonema, dizygotheca, *Dracaena deremensis, Ficus lyrata,* fittonia, spathiphyllum.

Minimum temperature 13°C. (55°F.) Adiantum, dieffenbachia, *Ficus elastica,* fittonia, kentia, maranta, neanthe, peperomia, phoenix, pilea, most philodendrons, platycerium.

Minimum temperature 7 to 10°C. (45 to 50°F.) Araucaria, *Cissus antarctica,* chlorophytum, euonymus, fatshedera, fatsia, hedera, rhoicissus, tradescantia.

For a sunny room with good ventilation: *minimum temperature 10 to 16°C. (50 to 60°F.)* Beloperone, bougainvillea, codiaeum, coleus, chrysanthemum, *Euphorbia splendens,* hibiscus, hippeastrum.

Minimum temperature 7°C. (45°F.) Azalea, cacti, *Campanula isophylla,* citrus, geranium.

For a room with some direct sun: *minimum temperature 16 to 18°C. (60 to 65°F.)* Anthurium, aphelandra, caladium, calathea, codiaeum, dracaena and cordyline, *Ficus benjamina.*

Minimum temperature 13°C. (55°F.) Asplenium, begonia, bromeliads, ceropegia, *Ficus elastica,* heptapleurum, impatiens, saintpaulia, schefflera, streptocarpus.

Minimum temperature 7 to 10°C. (45 to 50°F.) Achimenes, araucaria, asparagus, chlorophytum, cyclamen, *Euphorbia splendens,* grevillea, hedera, primula, rhoicissus, sansevieria.

For very cool winter conditions Acorus, araucaria, aspidistra, chlorophytum, fatshedera, fatsia, hedera, *Philodendron scandens,* tradescantia.

Plants for the office

Many offices with their adequate lighting and steady temperatures offer a seemingly ideal home for a number of plants and it is in these locations that the larger plants come into their own. The main problems come from the dryness of the air caused by central heating and/or air conditioning and public holidays and weekends which may make watering a difficulty.

Group plantings do much to counteract the lack of humidity and it is worthwhile purchasing a plastic sprayer for syringing particularly sensitive plants. On the whole, the tougher, leathery leaved plants such as monstera, ficus, peperomias and schefflera will survive best, along with the ever-popular Busy Lizzies, tradescantias, chlorophytum and African violets. With the exception of asplenium I have found the ferns impossible to maintain for any length of time but palms do well.

Buying the plants

House plants are steadily increasing in price and it is a waste of money as well as being disappointing if they die almost as soon as you get them home. So do shop around and be selective; the retailer who leaves the plants standing on the pavement where they are subjected to cold and winds is better avoided. The plants will suffer enough of a check from being moved from the closely controlled growing conditions of the grower's glasshouses to the retail area and then to your home, without the further handicap of being chilled and blown about. For this reason, too, make sure that the plants are adequately packed before they leave the shop. Summer is really the best time to make a purchase as plants are not subjected to such radical changes in temperature and there is less chance of acclimatization problems occurring.

Right
The splendid specimen of *Ficus benjamina* and the group arrangement of house plants on the table add character to a conference room

Below
Public buildings, such as this library, can be greatly enhanced by a well chosen display of plants

Left
A group of plants requiring special care; from left to right, *Scindapsus aureus* Marble Queen, *Ficus pumila*, *Dracaena deremensis rhoersii, Caladium* Red Flare, *Caladium candidum*

Above
Mme Auguste Haerens, a superb azalea which prefers coolish conditions and a steady temperature

Do's and Don'ts with Plants

As with any other living thing, plants need attention and care if they are to grow and look their best. An array of dusty, bedraggled and leggy specimens is no sort of ornament and unless you can set aside some time every week to attend to your plants then you will have to accept the fact that they are unlikely to give of their best. My collection at present numbers about 50 and it requires some two to three hours spread throughout the week to keep them looking good and growing well.

Watering

This is by far the most difficult and critical factor in house plant culture. Too many of us seem to reach for the watering-can as soon as a plant looks sick and all too often the problem has arisen from overwatering in the first place. Waterlogging the soil has the effect of driving all the air from the compost and, as oxygen is essential for good root growth, the roots become stunted and die.

Correct watering is, however, no easy task as it is impossible to stipulate an exact time and frequency; it is necessary to examine each plant and make an individual decision. If in any doubt it is much safer not to water. Do not be overcome by kindness and imagine that the plants need water every time you need a drink. Look at the compost, if it has a grey-brown appearance it is most likely to be in need of water. Check this by feeling about half an inch down into the compost. Soil which has come away from the sides of the pot is much too dry and it may require some effort to get it adequately moist as water runs straight through at the first application. Better to stand the pot in a deep container of water and leave it until the compost is thoroughly moist again.

The technique of watering is also important: use water at room temperature and fill the pot up, taking care not to splash the foliage or allow any water to lodge in the plant's centre. Never leave pots standing in dishes of water, any excess which trickles through should be discarded after a few minutes if it has not been absorbed into the pot. Watering from below is useful for plants such as African violet which do not like being splashed but I do not use this method as a general rule as it is so easy to overwater; stand the pot in a saucer of tepid water for about five minutes, after which any water which has not been absorbed should be thrown away.

In general, the warmer the conditions the more frequently will water be required but do remember that this applies equally to plants in the height of summer and those

Pot-bound plants in need of repotting

Similarly, stand the pots on pebbles in a tray or bowl containing water but make sure that the water is below the surface level of the pebbles and that the pots are not in contact with it. Standing pots on blocks of wood in a container of water is a variation of this and, once again, the water level should not reach the base of the pot.

Feeding

Plants which are growing well are less likely to be troubled by diseases or pests. However, composts soon become depleted of the nutrients essential for good growth and flower production and unless some form of supplementary feeding is given plants will suffer and cease to grow. In the main, feeding is required from early April to October, but any plant which grows or flowers in winter will require feeding then.

The easiest fertilizers to use are the proprietary ones manufactured especially for this purpose. Most need dilution and I cannot stress too much the importance of following the manufacturer's instructions – adding a spoonful 'for the pot' is not a good idea as all too often it can cause serious damage to the roots. I speak from some experience here – overfeeding my pet monstera because 'it looked as if it needed it' caused it to run wild and produce enormous ungainly leaves which spoiled its appearance and threatened the safety of visitors! Some fertilizers are available in dropper bottles which make application especially easy to judge.

Potting

Sooner or later you will be called on to perform this operation and it should be remembered that it is a fairly traumatic experience for a plant and many take some time to recover.

The spring is the best time for repotting existing plants when the roots are at their most active, and I check mine then to see if they are 'pot bound', which means that when knocked out of the pot the soil ball is covered with a mass of roots. Suspect this if roots can be seen growing from the drainage holes or if the plant has not been growing well. Certain plants, the aspidistra for one, prefer to be rather pot bound and should only be repotted once every few years. Other large plants may be impossible to handle and in such cases carefully remove an inch or two of compost from the surface and replace with fresh.

When selecting a new pot for the plant choose one which is only marginally bigger than that in which it is presently growing. Overpotting, the term for putting a plant into a much larger pot, usually results in delay in growth as the roots are forced to cope with too great an expanse of new compost.

For many years there have been discussions about the advantages or disadvantages of clay and plastic pots. For various reasons, plastic seems to have won the day. I seldom see clay ones offered for sale now and have found no marked difficulties in using the plastic kind, provided it is remembered that compost tends to dry out more slowly than in clay pots and watering must be done very carefully.

grown in a centrally heated room in winter; it does not necessarily follow that water should be drastically reduced in winter. In cooler conditions, however, much less water will be needed, and, as many plants require a winter rest when they are not growing, it is usually necessary to reduce the amount of water given in winter. Another guide line is the type of plant, those with harder or leathery foliage require less water than those with softer growth.

Watering during holiday periods, particularly in the summer, can be a problem unless you have a neighbour to whom you can entrust the task. There are also certain measures which may save the day: the pots can be well watered and stood on a layer of damp sand in bowls and/or packed around with damp newspaper; pots may be plunged to their rims in damp peat; glass fibre wicks can be used to connect the soil in the pot with a container of water, but soak the wick before use or it will not work. Smaller plants will survive if they are watered well and then sealed into a plastic bag. Whichever method you decide on always move the plants from sunny spots and keep them in the coolest, light place available. Do not be tempted to leave them standing in dishes of water.

Humidity

The provision of an adequately humid atmosphere is another factor which can greatly affect the plant's chance of survival. To improve local humidity, I find that a plant syringe is invaluable. This sprays a fine mist of water over the plants, and if used two or three times each day does much to counteract the effects of central heating. But this is not a remedy for use on hairy-leaved plants.

The ideal way of providing the necessary degree of humidity is to plunge the pots to their rims in a container of moist peat; this evaporates water in the vicinity of the plants, so increasing the moisture content of the air.

Above
An attractive bowl planted with hedera, *Neanthe bella*, saintpaulia, *Euonymus japonicus medio-pictus* and *Pilea cadierei nana*

Right
A group of plants with interesting foliage; from the top right in a clockwise direction are *Aglaonema* Silver Queen, *Hypocyrta glabra, Fittonia verschaffeltii, Scindapsus aureus, Maranta leuconeura kerchoveana* and *Peperomia caperata* Little Fantasy

Whichever pot you use it must be clean. The method of potting is shown in the accompanying illustrations.

Compost

The range of prepared composts for house plants is wide and it is mainly a matter of personal preference which you use. The chief distinction is between soil-based ones and soilless or peat-based kinds. The soil-based composts are heavier and I think preferable for larger plants or where weight is required to balance a heavy plant. The most usual soil composts are those with the prefix 'John Innes'. These are formularized mixtures of loam, peat and sand with added set amounts of fertilizers. There are three strengths, which relate to the quantity of fertilizer used,

Repotting a sansevieria. Carefully remove the plant from its pot by tapping this on the edge of a bench or table

After putting some compost in the base of the new pot, place the plant in position and these are known as John Innes potting compost No. 1, (J.I.P. 1), John Innes potting compost No. 2 (J.I.P. 2), and John Innes potting compost No. 3 (J.I.P. 3). When potting, the most appropriate strength is used; this is calculated on both the size and the rate of growth, larger plants in J.I.P. 2 or J.I.P. 3, smaller ones in J.I.P. 1. However, many house plants seem to grow better in a more open compost so try mixing 1 part by bulk of peat to 2 parts of the John Innes.

The soilless peat-based composts also contain fertilizers. When using these it is not necessary to firm the compost around the plants' roots to the same extent as with soil-based composts.

Gently trickle compost around the roots and firm it with the fingers or, if the space is too narrow, with a piece of wood as shown here

There should be at least half-an-inch of space between the surface of the compost and the top of the pot to allow room for watering

Above
Grouping plants in a trough of damp peat is the ideal way of increasing humidity in the immediate surroundings

Right
This range of interesting and easy plants includes, at the back from left to right, *Impatiens petersiana, Gynura sarmentosa, Beloperone guttata* and *Stephanotis floribunda.* In the front are *Tradescantia tricolor, Peperomia magnoliaefolia* and *Sedum sieboldii medio-variegatum*

Plant hygiene

Do you talk to your plants? It is perhaps not as ridiculous as it sounds – at least, when you talk to plants you tend to examine them closely and so are more likely to notice anything that is wrong and take prompt action to cure it.

Dusty plants always look neglected and unattractive. So do try to find time to sponge the leaves every few weeks with water to which a few drops of milk have been added. Sponging in this way helps to suppress insect pests as well as keeping the leaf pores clear of dust, but it should not be used on hairy-leaved plants; debris and dust can be removed from these with a very soft brush or pipe-cleaner.

There are a number of proprietary leaf gloss preparations on the market. These are good if used with care but beware of applying them too thickly as all too often this seals the leaf pores and causes the leaves to turn yellow and drop off. Some plants do not take kindly to such preparations and it is advisable to test one leaf first.

Left
Sponging a smooth-leaved plant to remove dust

Above
Cleaning dust from a hairy-leaved plant with a pipe-cleaner. A small paintbrush can also be used

Routine plant care involves checking each plant weekly, removing faded flowers and dead leaves and looking for any traces of insect pests or other signs of ill health.

The best insecticides for use on house plants are pyrethrum, derris and malathion (this should not be used on ferns). Pyrethrum will not harm human beings or animal pets and is the only one I would contemplate using in the house. I feel that other insecticides are safer used out of doors or in a garden shed. With all these chemicals do read the manufacturer's instructions and follow them implicitly, taking special care to keep all containers out of the reach of children. With good cultural techniques it is often possible to get by without having to resort to chemical control measures at all.

The chief plant troubles which may occur are:

Aphid The familiar garden greenfly can move indoors to make a mess of plants both by sucking sap from them and exuding the sticky honeydew which is an attractant for a fungus known as sooty mould. Spray with pyrethrum, derris or malathion. An alternative method, though not for hairy-leaved plants, is to wash the foliage in soapy water or in a solution of malathion. Wrap a piece of polythene around the top of the pot to stop the plant and soil from falling out and swish the foliage around in a bucket. Wear rubber gloves if using a solution of malathion.

Mealy bug and root mealy bug Both these pests are readily identifiable as they appear to be covered with white fluff and are to be found in the angles of stems, on leaves or on the roots. They are best removed by hand using a matchstick or toothpick topped with cotton wool soaked in methylated spirit or alcohol. Roots must be washed free of soil before being treated and the plant replaced in fresh compost.

Red spider mite This is most likely to be a problem in a dry, warm atmosphere. These tiny creatures are very difficult to see but suspect their presence if the leaves become mottled and dry looking. You may then be able to see fine webbing on the undersurfaces and the tiny red mites themselves with the aid of a lens. As this is essentially a problem connected with lack of humidity, frequent spraying with water directed particularly at the undersurfaces of the leaves will control it. If it has got a hold then spray with derris or malathion.

Scale insects These look like small brown or black hard blemishes on the veins of leaves and on stems. They are unsightly and the insects inside the scales damage the plants by sucking the sap. Remove by sponging with water or malathion – it may be necessary to use quite a lot of force to dislodge them.

A June display of flowering plants in a small conservatory

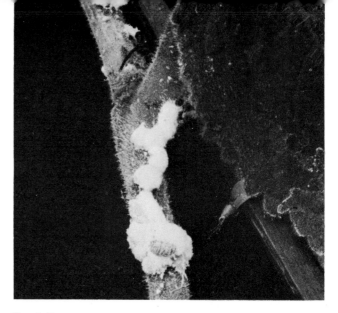

Top left
Washing a plant in a dilute soap solution is an effective control measure against aphids

Above
Mealy bug, a pest which may attack plants

Bottom left
Proprietary insecticides are available to control most house plant pests. They should be used with care

White fly Small white flies may sometimes be seen on the lower side of the leaves and on the stems. They suck the sap and may weaken plants considerably but are difficult to control and will require regular spraying with derris or malathion.

Rots and mildew Rotting stems or plant centres are usually a sign that some part of the cultural treatment is wrong. Check especially on overwatering. Remove all damaged parts and water sparingly. If too much of the plant has been affected then it is better to treat any sound pieces of growth as cuttings and destroy the remainder.

Mildew shows up as a white fungus on the stems and leaves and is brought about by overwatering, overcrowding or insufficient ventilation. Spray with a fungicide and improve the growing conditions.

On the whole, most things that go wrong with plants arise from bad or incorrect growing conditions, as all pests and diseases are most likely to attack and get a hold on plants which are not growing well. I have come from experience to expect most trouble from red spider with periodic attacks from greenfly. But in the case of the latter these are nearly always found to have been introduced on a flowering plant or bunch of flowers so inspect such floral tributes carefully before housing them in the same room as your other plants.

When faced with a sick plant look carefully to see if there are any signs of pests or diseases and take prompt action if any are found. Failing this you will have to do some detective work checking out and eliminating the most likely causes of the trouble. Check for over- or under-watering, draughts, sun scorch, a sudden change in temperature or light, too little light, frost damage, or damage from coal gas or other fumes.

General treatment for an ailing plant is to keep it on the dry side, in good light and an even temperature. Do not feed or repot it as this will aggravate the situation.

Plant Display

Plants growing in offices, homes, restaurants, hotels and other public buildings have become so much a part of modern living that we almost take their presence for granted. But it is interesting to see how well they complement much of modern interior design and provide a focal point in the expanse of an open-plan living or office area.

Their value was for many years recognized more clearly on the Continent where plants have for long been considered as an integral part of the home and have come to be displayed with a great deal of sophistication. I can remember when first going to work on a Danish nursery being impressed by the way the plants had almost grown into and become a part of the house instead of being perched around on any flat surface looking rather as if they weren't intending to stay.

Group planting

Too many single pots give rooms a cluttered, uncomfortable look. It is so much more interesting to try and group them together, allowing their various shapes to enhance each other for, curious though it may seem, plants enjoy each other's company as human beings do and thrive the better for it. A large array of containers, troughs and baskets is marketed and there should be no difficulty in finding one to suit any purpose. Troughs are especially useful for a position on a window-sill or in a window embrasure.

The plants can be arranged by either retaining them in their pots and simply plunging these in peat in the chosen container (which has the advantage of increasing humidity), or they can be removed from their pots and planted in compost. If you decide on the latter method, which, incidentally, does give more scope for placing plants at the most effective angle, be sure to select those with similar growing conditions. In any group arrangement use plants of varying heights, leaf form and colours. For example, choose one or two tall plants, such as *Ficus benjamina* and sansevieria, and underplant these with some of more bushy growth – *Begonia rex* and chlorophytum. Finally, add a couple of trailers to break the edge of the container: *Ficus pumila* and zebrina would be a good choice.

All house plants are better if displayed in groups, here the pots are plunged in a basket of peat

Above
An example of how plants have been used to complement
the appearance of a modern fireplace

Right
A light hall corner is a good setting for plants such as
Dieffenbachia Pia and *Hedera canariensis variegata*

An interesting innovation in group planting are Tower Pots – a system of pots which interlock one on top of the other to form a tower. There are two planting positions on opposite sides of each pot, so that if six pots are used there are twelve planting positions in the sides with one extra one in the centre of the top pot. I have been experimenting with one and it is proving very successful as well as looking increasingly attractive as the plants grow.

Cachepots

To improve the appearance of single pots many types of 'pot hiders' are available and these can be matched to surrounding furnishings or to the plant itself to create a feeling of unity. Apart from modern china, pottery and plastic ones try looking for jardinières in antique shops, especially if you have one of the Victorian favourites such as an aspidistra, rubber plant or maidenhair fern to house. Some of my most successful cachepots have been found among the selection of wastepaper baskets – wickerwork ones look good and have the advantage that they don't rust.

Wall brackets

Metal or wooden brackets supply a vantage point from which to trail such plants as chlorophytum, columnea, ceropegia, hedera, tradescantias, zebrina and *Scindapsus aureus*. The colour and pattern of the foliage look particularly effective against a plain wall.

Trellis

Consider, too, the possibility of an indoor trellis either
against a wall or used as a screen or room divider. Long
window-box containers hold the compost and furnish a
base for the trellis. Such a structure might be planted with
one of the vines – *Cissus antarctica* or *Rhoicissus rhomboidea* –
and a climber such as scindapsus or *Philodendron scandens*,
with some non-climbing plants to give substance at the
bottom.

Plant cabinets, Terrariums

For the real enthusiast there are special plant cabinets,
generally with fluorescent lighting and a built-in heating
system. These give complete control of the environment
and make it possible to grow the most difficult specimens
which will not survive under normal house conditions.
They are a modern development of the Wardian case
which was invented by Dr Nathaniel Ward in the early
19th century and used to transport plants safely on long
sea voyages. In essence these were simply metal- or
wooden-framed glass containers which were hermetically
sealed. The plants inside created their own atmosphere
and remained relatively unaffected by external conditions.

Terrariums are less elaborate plant cabinets and much
more nearly related to the Wardian case. In its simplest
form a terrarium is one plant growing in a glass container,
but terrariums are also miniature landscapes or arrangements of several plants. Many suitable containers can be
found; an old aquarium fitted with a covering sheet of glass
offers a lot of scope for an attractive piece of landscaping,
and, with a bit of ingenuity, many other objects such as
large balloon glasses, storage jars, goldfish bowls, sweet
jars and carboys can be pressed into service. A terrarium
in a bottle is also called a bottle garden and this can be as
much of a curiosity as a ship in a bottle and, in the case of
a narrow-necked bottle, almost as difficult to build.

When planting your chosen container, place a layer of
gravel in the bottom for drainage and then carefully pour
in some compost (either John Innes potting compost No.
1 with added peat or one of the peat-based kinds) through
a funnel made of paper. The depth used depends on the
height of the container and is varied to give a rise and
fall in the landscape. Choose small, slow-growing plants

Displayed in a corner of a garden room, from left to right, are codiaeum, *Dracaena deremensis rhoersii* with *Campanula isophylla* above, *Dracaena marginata tricolor*, *Scindapsus aureus* Marble Queen and, on the table, a sinningia

Tower Pots provide a lot of scope for interesting planting
Above
Planting up a terrarium in an old-fashioned sweet jar: the compost is poured into the container through a paper funnel
Left
A teaspoon is useful for making the planting holes

which like the warm humid conditions and plant these with the aid of a tiny trowel or spoon, working from the edge of the container to the centre. Use stones and pieces of bark to create a naturalistic effect.

To plant a narrow-necked bottle it is necessary to make a set of long-handled tools for manoeuvring the plants by tying a teaspoon and cotton reel to long canes. The teaspoon is used to dig the hole and the cotton reel to firm the plants in. Maintenance in this kind of terrarium presents something of a problem; to remove even a dead leaf requires some 'fishing' with a hook and razor blade attached to canes, but one does improve with practice.

With the exception of narrow-necked bottles, all containers should be covered to maintain the necessary moist humid atmosphere which is almost self-perpetuating. Terrariums need little water, possibly only a few times each year and are better left unfed.

Above
Pieces of stone carefully arranged add to the final effect

Top right
Finished terrariums in simple containers

Right
Firming plants in a narrow-necked bottle garden

Good plants for this purpose include adiantum, asplenium, calathea, cryptanthus, euonymus, *Ficus pumila*, fittonia, hedera, maranta, neanthe, peperomia, pilea, pteris, scindapsus, tradescantia, zebrina.

Garden room, Conservatory

A glassed-in extension which gives direct access to the house and provides not only a place for taking advantage of the sun in cool weather but also a good situation for growing many of the flowering pot plants and for giving some of the house plants a vacation in better light. Some kind of heating will be needed if you intend to keep plants there in the winter as well as plenty of allowance for ventilation and some provision for shading to guard against too hot conditions in summer.

Above
A decorative trough arrangement of tradescantia, chlorophytum, primula, *Begonia rex* and hedera

Right
Large plants, such as the *Monstera deliciosa* in the background and *Philodendron bipinnatifidum* in the foreground, need to be displayed in a spacious area to be seen at their best

Making New Plants

Sooner or later you may want to start increasing your own plants or growing new ones from cuttings other people offer you. Most of my own collection has been grown from 'swaps' of stem or leaf cuttings and it is quite an easy matter to raise plants in this way with a minimum of equipment. The basic requirement is for some kind of propagator which will provide the cuttings with the close and humid atmosphere they need if they are to root quickly and satisfactorily. This does not have to be costly – a wooden box covered with a sheet of glass would be suitable, or it is possible to purchase plastic seed trays which have transparent lids fitted with adjustable ventilators. For just a few cuttings a pot and plastic bag will suffice. A good rooting medium for use in the propagator is made by mixing equal parts by bulk of peat and coarse sand together.

Stem cuttings

These can be taken in spring if the propagating box has some method of heating otherwise it is better to wait until the summer. Choose a firm healthy stem and cut off a piece between 2 and 4 in. long, depending on the size of the plant. Try to make the cut below the point at which a leaf joins the stem. Trim off the lower leaves and insert

Top left
Cuttings of tradescantia being inserted in a pot of compost

Bottom left
The pot is placed inside a polythene bag to make a simple propagator

Above
Dracaenas can be increased from stem sections, which are potted individually

Right
Once rooted each section will produce plantlets from the dormant buds

the cuttings in the propagator or around the edge of a pot. Replace the lid of the propagator or put the pot into a plastic bag and tie the top. Keep the cuttings in a light place but not in direct sunshine. Inspect them every few days and remove any that may have rotted but do not disturb the others until fresh signs of growth can be seen, when they can be potted on individually. The process of rooting will be speeded up if the base of the cutting is dipped into hormone rooting powder before being inserted in the rooting medium. Water carefully if the rooting medium shows signs of drying out.

I have found that many cuttings will root very satisfactorily in a small glass of water and I often try this method first.

For plants with thick woody growth, cuttings are made from stem sections, each between 2 and 3 in. long and carrying at least one bud.

Left
All these plants can be increased by stem or leaf cuttings. From the left, *Sansevieria trifasciata laurentii* in the background with *Hedera helix* Adam and *Philodendron* Tuxla in front, *Bougainvillea* Killie Campbell behind *Euonymus japonicus medio-pictus* and *Philodendron scandens*. *Pilea cadierei nana* is in the right foreground

Above
Chlorophytum comosum variegatum can be easily increased by rooting the plantlets, while *Tradescantia fluminensis* Quicksilver can be propagated from cuttings

43

Leaf cuttings

A method of increase used for such plants as saintpaulia, sansevieria, streptocarpus and *Begonia rex*. Either the whole or part of the leaf is used, and, as for stem cuttings, some sort of propagator is required for rooting them. In the case of sansevieria, the long, sword-shaped leaf is cut into pieces about 1½ in. long, each piece being inserted in the propagator where it will eventually form roots and a shoot.

The colourful leaves of *Begonia rex* may be cut into squares of about an inch across. These are laid on the surface of the rooting medium and roots will form from the cut veins. Alternatively, the leaf may be kept entire but cuts made across the main veins on the undersurface. Once again the leaf is placed on the surface of the rooting medium and is held in position with pebbles or hairpins. Roots and small plants form at the cut veins.

For saintpaulia and streptocarpus, detach a leaf with a length of stem and insert this in the rooting medium, keep fairly warm if possible. Saintpaulia leaves can also be rooted in water: cover a small glass of water with foil or clear plastic wrap in which holes have been made for the leaf stems and suspend the stems so that about one-third of their length is in the water.

Above
Small plantlets produced on a leaf cutting of *Begonia rex*

Left
A leaf bud cutting of *Ficus elastica*. This should be inserted in a propagator

Top right
Saintpaulia leaf cuttings inserted in compost. Some have already produced small plants

Bottom right
Dividing a plant of sansevieria

Offsets

Bromeliads produce side shoots known as offsets at the base of their rosettes. These can be removed with a sharp knife and treated as cuttings.

Division

An easy method of increase for any plant which forms a number of crowns. The plant is knocked from its pot and the roots teased carefully apart so that it can be divided between the crowns or growing points.

Layering

A method which is used for plants with a trailing growth habit, e.g. hedera, scindapsus or philodendron. A slit is made into a node (the point where leaves join the stem) of a suitably placed shoot and the wounded area pegged down in a pot of compost. After roots have formed from the layer it can be detached from the parent plant.

The many forms of *Codiaeum variegatum pictum* are remarkable for their superb colourings

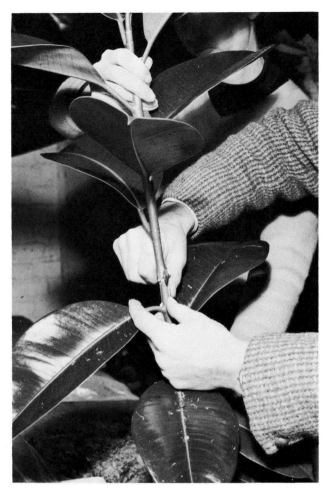

Air layering a rubber plant: first, a cut is made into the stem

Damp moss is placed around the wound

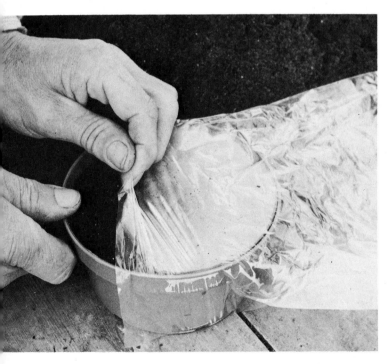

Covering a pot of seeds with a plastic bag to trap the warmth and moisture

Air layering

Sometimes known as Chinese layering, this offers a good way of rejuvenating a leggy specimen of rubber plant, monstera, fatsia or similar tall-growing plant which may loose its lower leaves. Choose a point towards the top of the plant and make a cut into the stem just below a leaf. Wedge the cut open with a matchstick, wrap some damp peat or sphagnum moss around the wounded area and secure it with thread. Then cover the peat or moss with a piece of plastic, binding this securely at the top and bottom with sticky tape. Roots will eventually form into the moss or peat and the plants can then be severed below the new root ball and potted up.

The remaining piece of plant will often produce a bud and shoot from lower down the stem.

Seed

Growing plants from seeds is very satisfying although it can also be a slow process, often taking a long time to get sizeable plants. The seeds are sown in seed trays of suitable compost and covered with a sheet of glass and piece of paper. Alternatively, they may be sown in a pot and placed inside a plastic bag. Once germination has occurred the coverings can be removed and the seedlings grown on until they are large enough to be moved to individual pots. This is usually when the first true leaves appear.

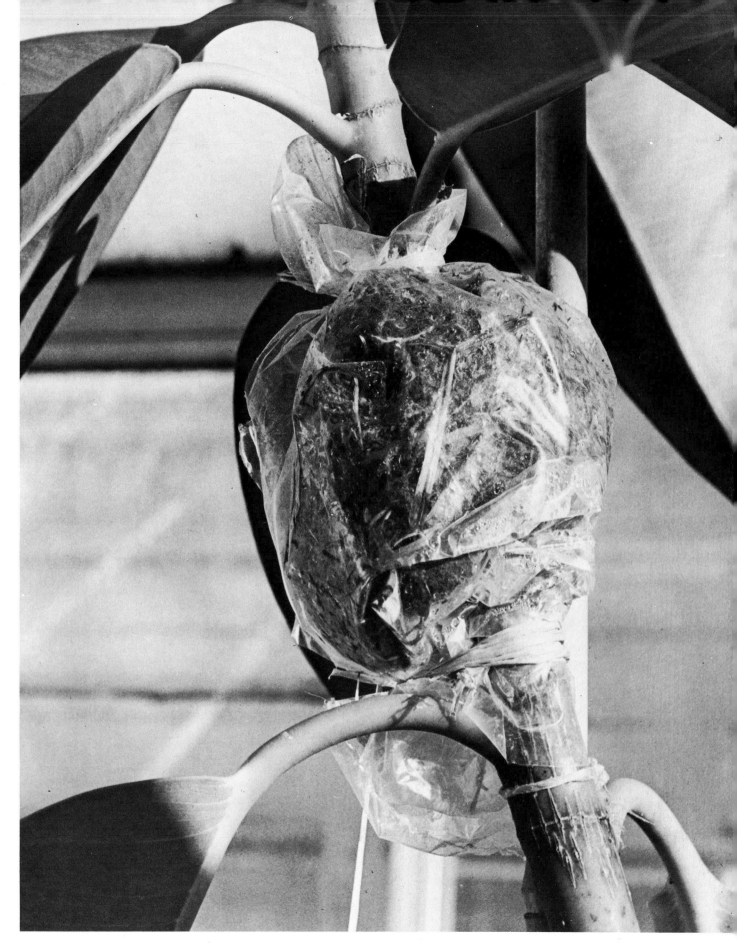

The moss is covered with a piece of plastic and well
secured

Above
A bowl arrangement containing *Cordyline terminalis* Red Edge, begonias, pteris and saintpaulia

Left
Attractive terrariums can be easily made in a variety of containers

Right
A corner of a conservatory containing *Fatsia japonica* (on the floor) with *Dracaena deremensis rhoersii* behind. The ledge at the back holds saintpaulia, *Scindapsus aureus* Silver Queen, sinningia and *Ficus pumila*. On the window-sill are cyclamen, platycerium and a selection of cryptanthus

An A to Z of Plants for All Tastes

Achimenes

Achimenes *Easy*

This pretty flowering plant has only one disadvantage in that it requires a resting period in winter. However, its flaring trumpet-shaped flowers of pink, mauve, red or deep purple, produced throughout a large part of its growing period, more than compensate for this.

Start the small scaly rhizomes into growth in February in a temperature around 10°C. (50°F.). Plant one inch deep, placing six rhizomes in each 5-in. pot. Water sparingly at first, then more freely as growth increases. Pinch the shoot tips frequently to encourage bushiness.

Keep the plants out of strong sunshine but in a well-lighted warm position.

The leaves die down naturally in autumn and the plant should then be allowed to dry off before being stored without watering in a warm, dry place for the winter. In February shake the rhizomes free from the old compost and start as previously described. Increase by breaking the rhizomes into pieces or sowing seed.

From left to right, *Ficus pumila*, codiaeum, *Acorus gramineus variegatus*

Acorus gramineus variegatus *Easy*

A plant with stiff, cream-striped, grass-like leaves which is useful for contrast in a mixed arrangement of plants or in bottle gardens. It may, however, be difficult to grow it successfully in such an arrangement for any length of time as it requires very moist and cool conditions and is at its best when grown in a pot which is kept standing in a deep saucer of water. It is a plant for a cool room and shady position. Increase by division when repotting.

Adiantum (Maidenhair Fern) *Not so easy*
Very dainty ferns, with wiry stems and delicate fronds, which are particularly good in bowl arrangements or hanging baskets. Give them a position out of the sun and away from draughts. Spray freely to maintain humidity. Keep well watered from spring to autumn without allowing the compost to become soggy and water very carefully in winter. Increase by division.

Adiantum raddianum

Anthurium (Flamingo Flower) *Needs special care*
These are not easy plants to grow as their main requirement is for constant moist heat, though *Anthurium scherzerianum* tolerates dry air better than *A. andreanum*. They need a light position, not in full sun, and should be watered and syringed freely in spring and summer, rather less frequently in autumn and winter. Use rain water if possible.

Aglaonema *Needs special care*

Plants with a fairly compact habit and elongated leaves marbled or patterned in white, green or silvery-grey. They require a warm, moist atmosphere with a minimum temperature of 16°C. (60°F.) and shade at all times. Give water in reasonable quantities in spring and summer but keep the compost barely moist in winter. Spray the leaves to maintain humidity or plunge the pots in peat. Feed during the growing season.

There are a large number of attractive species and varieties. Increase plants by division in spring or stem cuttings rooted in a warm propagator.

Aglaonema Silver Queen

Anthurium andreanum

The colourful spathes in pink or red, which give an impersonation of flowers, are produced in spring and early summer. Plants can be repotted in March and it is preferable to use a peat-based compost. When potting keep the crown above the compost and take care not to damage the aerial roots.

They can be propagated by division when repotting or by sowing seed in a warm propagator.

55

Above
Aphelandra squarrosa louisae

Anthurium scherzerianum

Aphelandra squarrosa louisae (Zebra Plant) *Not so easy*

A showy plant with dark green leaves boldly striped in white and usually bought when it is carrying its stiff spike of yellow flowers which lasts for many months. It needs a fairly light, draught-free position, warmth and humidity, and should be watered freely throughout the year and fed fortnightly. Shorten the stems after flowering to keep the bushy habit.

As a permanent house plant it should be regarded as a foliage plant only as it is unlikely to flower a second time under room conditions and really needs to be moved to a warm greenhouse after flowering.

Increase by cuttings in a warm propagator.

Araucaria excelsa (Norfolk Island Pine) *Easy*
This relative of the monkey puzzle makes a shapely tree of
100 ft. or more in suitable climates and I never cease to
marvel at the charming potted version which is one of
my favourite house plants. Grown in this way it is unlikely
to exceed 6 ft. so there should be no accommodation
problems.

It is really a display plant for a position where its dark
green needle-like leaves and branches in symmetrical
whorls will show to full advantage.

Araucaria prefers the cooler temperatures of 10 to
13°C. (50 to 55°F.), and a light position protected from
strong sunshine. Water well in spring and summer but
keep just moist in winter. This is a plant which will benefit
from being stood out of doors in a sheltered shady spot in
summer. Repot in spring and feed regularly in summer.
Increase by sowing seeds or take cuttings of young stems.

Araucaria excelsa

Asparagus *Easy*

There are two species of asparagus commonly cultivated as house plants and often incorrectly called ferns. These are *Asparagus plumosus*, with feathery foliage (often used by florists with cut flowers), and *A. sprengeri*, with narrow leaves and a trailing habit which makes it suitable for hanging baskets or for training up wires.

Grow both kinds in 5- or 6-in. pots in a peat-based compost and keep plants in a light position, though away from direct sunshine from late spring to autumn. Feed in summer and spray the leaves. Water freely in spring and summer, very moderately in autumn and winter when the minimum temperature required is 7°C. (45°F.). Repot every other year.

Increase by division when repotting or by sowing seeds in spring.

Asparagus sprengeri

Aspidistra elatior variegata

Aspidistra elatior

Aspidistra elatior (Cast Iron Plant, Parlour Palm) *Easy*

This long-suffering plant can withstand both poor light and a lot of neglect but is really seen at its best when well treated. Water freely in spring and summer, only moderately in autumn and winter and always allow the compost to become almost dry between waterings. Keep out of strong sunshine.

The leaves are great dust traps and should be sponged every few weeks with water containing a few drops of milk; such treatment will keep down any incidence of scale insect to which this plant is rather prone. With luck you may see the weird mauve and brown flowers which are sometimes produced at soil level. My plant has flowered regularly for a number of years, sometimes carrying as many as four flowers consecutively; however, I find them rather repulsive and of curiosity value only.

There is a white-striped form which is more attractive although it is also more demanding and will not put up with any neglect.

Only repot aspidistras when absolutely necessary; it is better to replace some of the top soil each year instead. Increase by division when repotting.

Asplenium nidus (Bird's Nest Fern) *Not so easy*

A lovely fern for the house. The clear green shining fronds arranged like a shuttlecock are almost translucent when seen in good light and being slightly heavier and thicker than the fronds of the maidenhair ferns are able to withstand the dryer conditions of most homes rather better.

It prefers some warmth, to be out of direct sunshine and in a moist atmosphere; the fronds become deformed unless adequate humidity is maintained. I make a point of spraying the fronds and centre of my plant at least twice a day and it repays this attention with a constant succession of new fronds. Water freely throughout the year and keep away from draughts. Do not use any leaf-cleaning agents on the fronds.

Asplenium nidus

Begonia masoniana

Begonia *Not so easy*

There is a range of begonias for indoor cultivation, but the foliage plants described below are the kinds most widely available.

Begonia rex deserves to be popular with its large, lopsided, heart-shaped leaves magnificently marked in crimson, green, silver, grey and black. There are a number of strains each varying in the colour combinations of the markings and I usually have difficulty in making a choice between them.

They do well in a peat-based compost and need to be watered freely from late spring to early autumn, fed fortnightly and kept in a light, draught-free position. Try also to maintain a good level of humidity, preferably by plunging the pots in peat. Water sparingly in winter. Repot in spring as plants do not do well if they are pot bound. Increase by division in spring when repotting or by leaf cuttings in summer.

Begonia masoniana is similar in form to *B. rex* but has corrugated green leaves each carrying a distinctive brown marking from which it gets its common name of the Iron Cross Begonia. It is grown in the same way as *B. rex*.

Right
Forms of *Begonia rex*

Beloperone guttata (Shrimp Plant) *Easy*

The common name is derived from the colour and shape of the bracts which accompany the small white flowers.

Water plants fairly freely in spring, summer and autumn but keep almost dry in winter and in a cooler place. It is sometimes difficult to get plants to flower, and what is needed is a minimum temperature of 10°C. (50°F.) with high humidity. They also need to get some direct sunshine and to be fed regularly. Remove the growing tips to encourage branching and cut the plant back when it becomes leggy, using the shoot tips as cuttings. This is a plant which is better when raised afresh from cuttings each year.

Beloperone lutea is a rarer species with greenish yellow bracts. It needs the same treatment.

Beloperone guttata

Bougainvillea *Easy*

These spectacular plants with flowers (really bracts) of magenta, pink, red or orange will grow out of doors in warm climates but do not survive frost. They are good plants for a garden room or any sunny, airy position and should be grown in large pots with the stems trained to canes or wires. Water freely in spring and summer, rather sparingly in autumn and keep almost dry in winter. Feed regularly in summer with weak fertilizer.

Bougainvillea Mary Palmer

Rest plants in winter in a cool, frost-free place and in March remove overcrowded stems, shorten side shoots to a few inches and move into a greenhouse or room with a higher temperature. Gradually increase the water supply to start plants into growth. Increase by cuttings rooted in a propagator.

65

Bromeliads *Easy*

A group of striking plants each with a rosette of leathery recurving leaves which are often beautifully marked. Many grow large and need a lot of room to be seen at their best. Some kinds have a 'vase' in the centre of the rosette and it is from here that the flowers are produced.

Bromeliads do best if grown in the smallest pots which will contain their roots potted either in a mixture of equal parts of peat, sand and osmunda fibre, or John Innes potting compost No. 2 and peat in equal quantities. Keep them in good light, away from direct sunshine, and maintain a moist atmosphere. The compost needs to be moist but never overwet and the vase, if present, must be kept filled with fresh water – rain water if possible. Feed fortnightly in summer. Some of the most widely available bromeliads are described below and on page 68.

Aechmea (Urn Plant) The species mostly seen is *Aechmea fasciata* which has green leaves covered with grey scales and banded in silver white. This plant takes a long time to produce and is best bought when the spike carrying the head of rose-coloured bracts is just above the level of the water in the central vase. Small blue flowers appear between the bracts and when the cluster of bracts and flowers dies, which will not be for several months, remove the stem just above the water level. Unfortunately, each rosette produces only one stem of flowers before it dies. However, by the time this happens side shoots will have grown around the base and these can be used to propagate the plant. Cut off the old rosette above the level of the side shoots and either pot on the whole plant or divide and repot the side shoots separately.

Top left
This log has been planted with *Cryptanthus fosteriana* (at the top) and *C. bromelioides tricolor*

Above
Aechmea fasciata

Topping up the 'vase' of a bromeliad with water

Ananas comosus variegatus Out of all the species of ananas this, the variegated pineapple, is an exceptionally striking plant with cream-edged serrated leaves which make a startling contrast to the head of vibrant pink bracts produced from the centre. A good plant for the garden room. Treat as for aechmea after the flower stem dies.

Billbergia nutans This is a smaller type of bromeliad with stiff narrow leaves about 12 in. high. In summer arching stems carrying drooping green, yellow and blue flowers surrounded by pink bracts appear but these are not as spectacular as they sound. Plants need to be pot bound to flower.

This is one of the easiest to grow as it will tolerate cooler temperatures and dryer air than the others. It is propagated by offsets.

Cryptanthus (Earth Stars) Small bromeliads with flattened rosettes of leaves looking a little like starfish. There are various species with leaves in a range of colours and beautifully mottled, cross banded or striped. All are good plants for a bottle garden. Look out for *Cryptanthus bromelioides tricolor*, with leaves striped in pink, cream and green and *C. zonatus zebrinus*, with bronzy purple leaves with silver crossbands, among others.

Neoregelia carolinae tricolor A very striking rosette of cream- and pink-striped green leaves which turns scarlet in the centre when it is about to flower. The small blue flowers are produced almost at water level in the central vase and the rosette dies after flowering when the plants can be treated as for aechmea.

Vriesea Bromeliads with very beautiful foliage, banded and mottled in different designs. *Vriesea splendens* is often seen, the dark green leaves cross banded in brown with a spike of scarlet bracts which maintain their colour for a long time although the leaves tend to lose their markings once the flowers are produced.

Ananas comosus variegatus

Vriesea fenestralis

Caladium *Needs special care*

Very decorative foliage plants with shield-shaped leaves mottled and marked in green, white, pink and red. They need a temperature of 18 to 24°C. (65 to 76°F.) with a moist atmosphere and good light to develop the colour in the leaves but they must be shaded from strong direct sunshine. Water carefully when the plants are growing, allowing the compost to dry a little between waterings. In autumn, reduce the amount of water and keep almost dry in winter in a temperature of about 13°C. (55°F.). To start the tuberous roots into growth in spring pot in a peat-based compost and keep the pots in a temperature of at least 20°C. (68°F.). Water sparingly at first and then freely as growth begins.

Because of their heat requirement these are not easy plants to keep from one year to the next and it may be better to consider them as expendable, buying them to enjoy during the four months or so when they will look their best.

Left
Mixed forms of *Caladium bicolor*

Above
Calathea makoyana

Calathea *Needs special care*

Relatives of maranta, these are pretty foliage plants with oval leaves, blotched and marked with darker green and often with dark red undersurfaces. They should be grown in a peat-based compost which is freely draining and need warm, humid, shady conditions. Good plants for the bottle garden or other terrariums, in fact, they are difficult to grow well anywhere else.

Water well in summer but keep much dryer in winter, feed in summer and spray with water or plunge pots into peat to maintain the necessary humidity. The tips of the leaves go brown if the compost remains wet and cold for any length of time. Increase by division.

Campanula isophylla

Campanula isophylla *Easy*

This trailing perennial with blue or white star-shaped flowers is useful for hanging baskets and can be trained upwards against a suitable support. It will tolerate a range of temperatures if well watered and fed regularly but is at its best out of strong sunshine in fairly cool humid conditions.

Water normally but never allow the compost to dry out as this causes shrivelling of the leaves. The flowers are carried from July to the end of September and plants need feeding during the flowering period. After flowering cut back and keep dryer over winter in a very cool temperature, 4°C. (40°F.). Increase by division in spring or by cuttings.

Ceropegia woodii (Hearts Entangled) *Easy*

Not a striking plant but an unusual one which never fails to attract attention with its small grey-green heart-shaped leaves from which it gets its common name. It also produces strange white and purple flowers but these are not particularly attractive.

The thread-like growths do get easily tangled and, therefore, this is a plant which is seen at its best if placed on a shelf or wall bracket from which the growths can hang. I have also seen it used most effectively hanging in front of a window. It needs a light position and should be kept on the dry side.

Increase from cuttings of the thin twining growth rooted in peat, or by layering. Older plants produce small white knobbly tubers along the length of the stem and these can be used for propagation if removed with a length of growth and rooted in peat.

A display of very decorative plants which includes
Ficus benjamina (left), *Dizygotheca elegantissima* (top
right), codiaeums and a variety of *Hedera helix*

Chlorophytum comosum variegatum

Chlorophytum (Spider Plant) *Easy*

Well-grown specimens of this can look striking with their large tufts of narrow leaves striped in cream and green. Long arching stems are produced with small white flowers and plantlets which can be rooted easily when pegged into soil or detached and rooted in water.

These are very tolerant plants which will grow in cool or warm rooms though the ideal is about 13°C. (55°F.). Water freely in spring and summer, moderately in autumn and winter and feed in summer. It is difficult to prevent the leaf tips going brown but to improve the appearance either snip these off or remove the whole leaf. This problem will be helped if the plant is fed regularly and repotted as soon as it requires it.

Cissus antarctica (Kangaroo Vine) *Easy*

A very easy and tough plant with attractive, glossy, notched leaves and a climbing habit which comes in handy for providing contrast in a group planting. It supports itself by tendrils and should be given canes or a trellis on which to climb.

This is really a plant for a cool room and good light but it can be grown in sun or a certain amount of shade although at higher temperatures the leaves may turn brown. Water freely in spring and summer, moderately in autumn and winter and feed in summer. Pinch shoot tips occasionally in summer to induce a more bushy habit. Increase by cuttings.

Citrus mitis (Calamondin Orange) *Not so easy*

Citrus mitis

This is the best orange for indoor cultivation as it has a good compact habit and will produce fruit when quite a small plant. The white fragrant flowers are carried in spring and early summer.

It needs a well-lighted window and should, if possible, be stood out of doors in summer in a warm, sunny place as sunshine is necessary to ripen the growth and ensure flowering and fruiting. Water freely in spring and summer, moderately in autumn, sparingly in winter, and feed when the plant is producing new leaves. Plants can be pruned after flowering if necessary. Watch out for scale insects which may be troublesome. Increase by cuttings in summer or by sowing the pips.

Codiaeum variegatum pictum reidii

Codiaeum (Croton) *Needs special care*

Most of the crotons have oval or lance-shaped leaves mottled in green, yellow, red, orange, black and bronze, but there are some species with very narrow leaves and these tend to be easier to manage than the others.

The basic need is for steady warmth, humidity and ample light to maintain the leaf colours. Pot in spring, feed in spring and summer and also in winter if leaves are being produced. Water moderately in winter and maintain a temperature of around 16°C. (60°F.). Watch for red spider if conditions become hot and dry and spray the foliage with water. Increase by cuttings in a warm propagator in summer.

Coleus *Easy*

Brilliant foliage plants in shades of red, yellow, pink and green in various combinations. Grow in a light position with some sunshine. They will need plenty of water in summer and should be fed regularly. Water more sparingly in the winter. Pot on as necessary and pinch growth frequently to maintain a bushy habit.

Increase is easy from cuttings rooted in compost or water, or from seeds. I was fascinated last year when growing a batch from seed to find how early the foliage colours become differentiated. This is, in fact, at the first true leaf stage and it is possible then to make a selection of the best colour combinations.

Colourful forms of coleus

78

Left
Columnea gloriosa

Below
Dieffenbachia exotica

Columnea *Needs special care*

Trailing plants, especially useful for hanging baskets, with small leaves and red or orange tubular flowers which are freely produced under the right conditions of constant warmth and humidity – requirements which may be difficult to supply in the average home.

Pot in a peat-based compost, keep in a semi-shady place and take care when watering never to allow the compost to become saturated. Increase by cuttings rooted in a warm propagator.

Dieffenbachia (Dumb Cane) *Not so easy*

The common name derives from the unpleasant smelling sap which, if it gets into the mouth, will cause considerable pain, irritation and swelling. The large oval leaves, with their markings in cream or yellow and green are very decorative.

This is a plant for a shady, warm position with a minimum winter temperature of 16°C. (60°F.). Water freely in spring and summer, very moderately in autumn and winter. Feed in summer and spray the leaves with water.

Increase by cuttings of stem sections rooted in a warm propagator.

Dracaena and Cordyline *Not so easy*

The main distinguishing feature of these two groups of plants is the arrangement and type of flowers. However, as most nurserymen seem to market all of them as dracaena it is easier to deal with them under one heading.

They are all rather difficult to please, requiring warmth and humidity. Water well in summer but very carefully in winter, allowing the soil to dry out a little between waterings. Use rain water or soft water if you can. Feed during the summer and keep plants in a good light, though out of strong sunshine.

All are plants with very handsome foliage; my favourite is *Dracaena marginata tricolor*, the rainbow plant, which makes a graceful fountain of grass-like recurving leaves striped cream and green with pinky red margins. This has the bonus of being an easier plant as it needs less warmth than the others.

Dracaena marginata tricolor

Dizygotheca elegantissima

Dizygotheca elegantissima *Needs special care*

Also listed as *Aralia elegantissima*, this plant is a very dainty individual with bronzy-green, narrow, serrated leaves. Like a number of elegant plants it is rather choosy about its growing conditions and needs fairly constant warmth, a shady position and humid atmosphere – plunge the pot in peat if you can and spray the leaves frequently. It must always be watered carefully as it does not like standing in wet compost. Increase by cuttings in summer.

Euonymus *Easy*

Perhaps more familiar as a garden shrub but it also makes a useful pot plant for a cool well-ventilated and light situation. Water moderately at all times and watch for attacks of mildew.

Euonymus japonicus medio-pictus is specially attractive; the oval, waxy leaves are green at the edge with a golden yellow splash in the centre and the yellow is continued down the petiole and the stem, giving the whole plant a rather fresh look.

Increase by cuttings.

Euphorbia pulcherrima, red, pink and white forms

Euphorbia pulcherrima (Poinsettia) *Not so easy*

A well-known and popular Christmas plant with large bracts in red, pink or white. Water moderately in autumn and winter and keep in good light in a minimum temperature of 13°C. (55°F.). After the bracts die reduce the water supply and keep nearly dry for a few weeks. Then, in early spring, cut the stems back by two-thirds, restart watering and move the plants into a temperature of around 18°C. (65°F.). This will encourage the production of new growth, which is most attractive both in shape and in its clear green colour. Keep the plant in a light, sunny position and water freely.

It is difficult to make the plant produce its coloured bracts under average home conditions as to do so requires special treatment to control the day length – giving no artificial light after natural daylight hours from mid-September to December. However, even without its bracts, it makes a most handsome foliage plant.

Increase by cuttings of young shoots rooted in a propagator.

Euphorbia splendens (milii) (Crown of Thorns) *Easy*

In contrast to the poinsettia this is a stiffly branching plant with rather wicked thorns, small, oval leaves and red flower-like bracts produced in liberal quantities. Grow it in good light with some direct sunshine. Water reasonably well in spring and summer, though flowers are more usually produced if the compost is kept slightly dry. Water only sparingly in autumn and winter.

It can be increased from stem cuttings which should be allowed to dry for 24 hours or so before being inserted in sandy compost in a propagator. Remove the tips from young plants to encourage branching.

All euphorbias contain a white, milky sap which is poisonous and should not be allowed to get near the mouth or eyes.

Fatshedera lizei *Easy*

A cross between *Fatsia japonica* and *Hedera helix* (ivy) with attractive leaves and an upright stem which needs pinching if you want the plant to branch. Grow it in a peat-based compost in a slightly shady, coolish place although it can be acclimatized to higher temperatures. There is a form with cream-edged leaves which needs more heat.

Increase by rooting the top of the plant or pieces of the stem.

Fatshedera lizei variegata

Fatsia japonica *Easy*

Also known as *Aralia sieboldii* and often mis-named the
castor oil plant, this is a very tough plant with shining
green leathery leaves which can be grown in unheated
rooms or even out of doors. It makes a tall plant and
should be pinched back to keep it bushy. Feed regularly
and water freely in summer, moderately in winter. Red
spider is likely to be a problem in dry conditions.

There is a form of this with cream-variegated leaves,
but this is more difficult to obtain and rather more
difficult to grow.

Increase the species by seed, the variegated form by
cuttings.

Fatsia japonica variegata

Ficus (Fig) *Range from easy to needing special care*
This genus includes a number of very useful plants including the ever-popular rubber plant.

Ficus benjamina (Weeping Fig) My favourite plant in this genus, the small glossy green leaves and weeping habit make it a good choice for group planting. Use a peat-based compost and do not overpot. Water carefully, never allowing the compost to dry right out.

There may be some problems with acclimatization and until the plant becomes accustomed to its new environment the leaves may go yellow and fall off.

Ficus elastica (Rubber Plant) This was a favourite plant of the Victorians and is still very popular today. A fairly robust plant which will grow in poor light but is better in good light with some sunshine. A minimum temperature of 13°C. (55°F.) is recommended but the green-leaved varieties will survive at 10°C. (50°F.). Water fairly freely from mid-spring to early autumn and then sparingly; this is a plant which should never be overwatered. Feed in summer and sponge the leaves occasionally.

Ficus elastica robusta is an improved variety of the old faithful. *F. elastica doescheri* and *F. e. schryvereana* are variegated forms with leaves in a range of colours – green, grey and creamy-yellow.

Ficus lyrata (Fiddle-leaved Fig) Rather like the rubber plant in appearance but the large light green leaves have a waist – hence the common name – and might be considered to be more decorative. It is also a more difficult plant as it will not grow well in varying temperatures and needs winter warmth (16°C., 60°F.). Water carefully and keep in good light but out of direct sunshine.

Ficus pumila (Creeping Fig, Climbing Fig) With its tiny round green leaves and trailing habit it is hard to believe that this is a relative of the rubber plant. It is fast growing, needs good watering all the time and feeding in spring and summer. Grow in a shady position, and pinch out the tips to encourage branching.

Ficus radicans Another trailing or climbing plant which has larger leaves than *F. pumila*, attractively variegated in cream in *F. radicans variegata*. This is a plant which is very sensitive to dry air and is, therefore, a good choice for the terrarium. Another way of growing it successfully is to allow it to climb up a pillar of netting packed with damp moss. Spray frequently with water.

Increase *F. elastica* and *F. lyrata* by air layering and these and all the others by stem cuttings rooted in a warm propagator.

Ficus elastica doescheri

Ficus elastica decora

Ficus radicans variegata

Ficus lyrata

Grevillea robusta

Fittonia *Needs special care*

Low-growing plants with leaves handsomely marked in red or silver which do best in bottle gardens and other terrariums where they can be given the warmth and humidity they need. Otherwise pot them in a peat-based compost, and keep in a draught-free position out of strong sunshine with a minimum temperature of 13°C. (55°F.). Increase the humidity by plunging pots in peat and spraying the leaves. Take care not to overwater, particularly in winter.

Plants can be increased by division in spring or by stem cuttings.

Grevillea robusta (Silk Oak) *Easy*

A beautiful tree which I much admired when in its native Australia, this makes an elegant fast-growing plant with silvery, fern-like leaves which can quickly become something of an embarrassment indoors. It is easily grown from seeds sown in spring and so might be regarded as expendable when it does get too big – if you can harden your heart!

Keep it in a light, airy position, standing it out of doors in summer if you wish. Water well in spring and summer, moderately in autumn and winter; it should never be allowed to dry out.

Fittonia argyroneura

Below *Gynura sarmentosa*

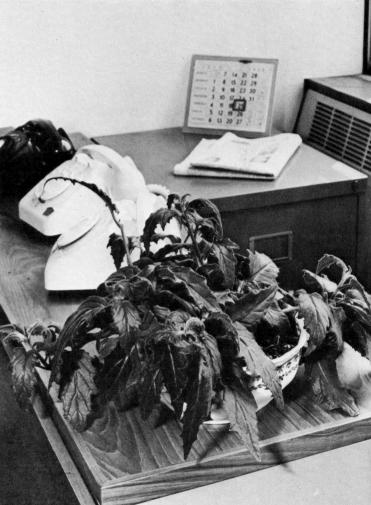

Gynura sarmentosa *Easy*

This trailing plant with purple velvety stems and leaves is tremendously eye catching – I have always had a waiting list for cuttings.

It needs a reasonably light position and should never be overwatered. Pinch the tips frequently to encourage bushiness. If left to itself it will produce unattractive ragged orange flowers which have an unpleasant smell and are better removed. In time plants become straggly and lose a lot of their colour and it is better to start again from cuttings, which can be easily rooted in a propagator or in water.

Hedera helix Chicago *variegata*

Hedera (Ivy) *Easy*

This large group of hardy climbing and trailing plants contains many useful varieties for group planting.

Ivies are very easy to grow indoors and are adaptable to a wide range of conditions though they do not do well in higher temperatures. Ideally, they should be in a light position, particularly the variegated kinds. Water well in spring and summer, moderately in autumn and winter and keep the atmosphere moist to prevent attacks of red spider. Feed regularly when plants are growing.

Many of the kinds offered are varieties of *Hedera helix* and there is such a choice of colours that it is really a case of looking and choosing the ones which appeal to you.

Hedera canariensis and its variegated form have larger leaves and are more tolerant plants for warmer rooms.

All the ivies can be grown from cuttings, which will often root in water.

Hedera canariensis variegata

Heptapleurum arboricola

Heptapleurum arboricola (Parasol Plant)
Easy

This elegant and fast-growing plant is so lovely I do advise you to look for it. The common name comes from the shape of the dark green leaves each of which is made up of a whorl of 9 or 10 stalked leaflets. An ideal plant for use as a specimen for display.

Keep it in good light with shade from direct sun, and water moderately all the year. Spray the leaves occasionally with water, frequently if the atmosphere is hot and dry.

The top can be pinched out to make it branch and this will give a better size of plant for a limited space.

Increase by seed or cuttings.

Hibiscus rosa-sinensis *Easy*

A plant worth growing for the exotic trumpet-shaped single or double flowers in brilliant colours – red, pink, yellow and salmon. Although each flower only lasts for a day the flowering period is a long one; in fact, flowers can be carried throughout the summer if a steady temperature can be maintained. Bud dropping may occur in fluctuating temperatures and if the plant is placed in a draught.

Keep it in a light, sunny position, water freely in spring and summer, sparingly in autumn and winter and feed regularly during the flowering period. Spray the leaves occasionally with water and watch for attacks of red spider.

The plant does not have an attractive habit as it tends to become straggly but it will stand fairly severe cutting back in spring. Increase by cuttings rooted in a warm propagator.

Hibiscus rosa-sinensis hybrids

94

Hippeastrum

Hippeastrum *Easy*

A bulbous plant which grows quickly and produces enormous trumpet flowers on stems some 2 ft. tall. The bulbs are expensive but as the flowers are so spectacular it is worth trying one.

Some bulbs are specially prepared for Christmas flowering and these should be potted in autumn using pots slightly larger than the bulb and inserting this to half its depth in the compost. Water sparingly until growth is well under way and then increase. Ordinary bulbs can be potted from January to March and treated in the same way.

Continue to water and feed occasionally after the flowers die to encourage full development of the leaves. From early September reduce the water until the leaves die. Keep the bulbs dry until growth is restarted in late winter or spring.

Hypocyrta glabra

Below Variegated form of *Impatiens wallerana*

Hypocyrta glabra (Clog Plant, Goldfish Plant) *Easy*

The common names arise from the orange, pouched-shaped flowers produced in summer. This is a compact plant with thick round glossy leaves which prefers a light position. Water normally and pinch the tops of shoots in spring or late summer if necessary. Increase by cuttings in summer.

Impatiens (Busy Lizzie) *Easy*

Very popular flowering plants with bright red, pink, white or bicoloured flowers produced throughout the year in adequate warmth.

The plants need a warm, moist position and they must be watered well in spring and summer and fed regularly. Red spider may be a problem if the atmosphere becomes too dry. Water only moderately in autumn and winter and keep warm and light if plants are to survive the winter in good condition.

Pinch stems back when necessary to encourage bushiness and use the shoots removed as cuttings. These will root easily in water.

96

Kentia belmoreana

Kentia belmoreana *Easy*

More correctly called *Howeia belmoreana* but still often offered for sale under its old name. This handsome palm is so well liked by interior designers that it is widely used for display in offices, shops and restaurants.

It is an easy plant tolerating poorer light than other palms and some neglect, and it will eventually reach a good height though this will take many years. It will be happy if potted firmly in good compost. Keep evenly moist but on the dry side if conditions are cool. It can be grown from seed but takes a long time to mature.

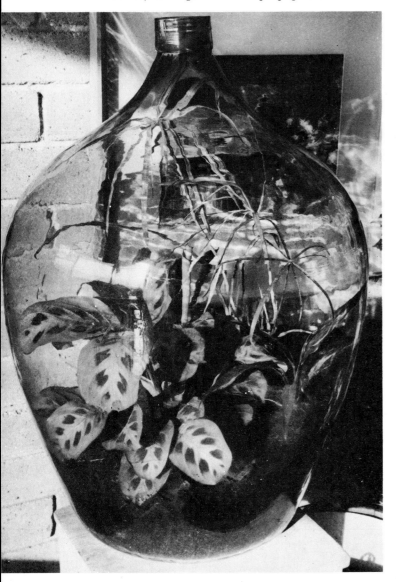

Maranta leuconeura erythrophylla

Maranta (Prayer Plant) *Not so easy*
Small plants with interesting leaf markings which need
constant warmth and humid conditions. Pot in a peat-
based compost and keep out of direct sunshine. Water
moderately most of the year giving a little more in summer.
Spray the leaves and take other measures to increase the
humidity. The leaves go brown at the tips if the plant is
grown in cold, wet compost. Like the calatheas these
are good plants for bottle gardens and other terrariums.

The common name refers to the leaves which fold
together in the evening. *Maranta leuconeura kerchoveana* is
the most usual kind with light green leaves each marked
with two rows of dark blotches. The more striking *M.l.
erythrophylla* has yellow-green leaves patterned with dark
red veins.

Increase by cuttings in a warm propagator.

Maranta leuconeura kerchoveana is often seen at its best
when grown in a bottle garden

Monstera (Swiss Cheese Plant) *Easy*

Another very popular and good display plant with attractively cut and perforated leaves. The number of perforations present depends on the age of the plant.

It needs good light to grow well but should be kept out of strong sunshine. Winter warmth with a minimum temperature of 10°C. (50°F.) is required and plants must be watered with care, allowing the compost to dry out a little between waterings. Feed from late spring to the end of summer. Keep out of draughts and away from fluctuating temperatures. Sponge the leaves frequently to keep them clean. The aerial roots which hang down from the stem should be trained into the pot and not cut off.

Monstera deliciosa

Neanthe bella

Neanthe bella (Chamaedorea elegans)
Easy

Small, neat, slow-growing palms which are good for terrariums and also for display. I have one which is thriving in a group arrangement – even to the extent of producing sprays of small flowers.

As is the case with all the palms, neanthe needs a freely draining compost, is best in a light position, though not in full sun, and a minimum temperature of 13°C. (55°F.). The leaf tips will go brown in a hot, dry atmosphere or when the plant is grown in cold, wet compost.

Water freely in spring and summer, sparingly in autumn and winter and sponge the leaves occasionally while keeping a good watch for scale insects.

Pachystachys lutea (Lollipop Plant) *Needs special care*

An interesting plant with dark green leaves and stiff cones of orange-yellow bracts. Grow it as for aphelandra but give it more warmth with a minimum temperature of 16°C. (60°F.). Feed and water well.

Increase by cuttings of a pair of leaves with a piece of stem.

Pachystachys lutea

Pandanus veitchii (Screw Pine) *Easy*

A good palm-like plant for a position which shows its
fountain-like shape to advantage. The spiny recurving
leaves are green with a white or cream margin and are
arranged in a spiral formation arising from a central stem.

Moist, warm conditions (minimum temperature 13°C.,
55°F.) are required and light. Spray the leaves regularly,
water freely in summer and feed fortnightly. Water
sparingly in winter.

Propagate from suckers which grow at the base.

Pandanus veitchii

Pelargonium (Geranium) *Easy*

A regal pelargonium, variety Sienna

This is the correct name for the tender greenhouse plants commonly called geranium and widely used for summer bedding displays and in garden rooms. These plants need a lot of light in summer or they become leggy so are better placed out of doors or in a well-ventilated conservatory.

There are numerous types classified roughly as: Zonal leaved, with interesting leaf markings and white, red, pink, or purple flowers carried for much of the year; Regal, with large beautiful spring flowers; Ivy leaved, with a trailing habit which is useful for hanging baskets, and the Scented leaved, with aromatic foliage in a range of delicate fragrances – lemon, orange, apricot, apple, lime – but these are rather straggly and have nothing to recommend them for general display.

It is possible to keep the plants from one year to the next but they are better if raised afresh each year from cuttings taken in spring or autumn and rooted in sand.

Rehouse the plants in early autumn and keep them fairly dry in cool but frost-free conditions for the winter. Cut back in spring, start watering more freely and move into a warmer place.

Peperomia magnoliaefolia

Peperomia *Easy*

Smallish plants with slightly fleshy ornamental leaves, often with pink or red stems. Flowers may be produced in warm, moist conditions but these are not particularly attractive.

They are better grown in peat-based compost and kept in a moist atmosphere with shade from strong sunshine. Water carefully at all times as plants have a tendency to rot, and spray the leaves occasionally. Repotting is seldom necessary as they get a lot of their food from the air. They are good plants for bottle gardens and other terrariums.

There are a large number of species, some of which are attractively variegated.

Increase is by leaf or stem cuttings.

Philodendron bipinnatifidum

Philodendron *Not so easy*

Many of these are quick-growing climbers. They produce aerial roots and will grow well on pillars of netting filled with damp moss. Most are fairly easy to grow and reasonably tolerant but will do best in warmth and humidity, so pots should be plunged in peat if possible. Use a peat-based compost and make sure the plants are in a shady, draught-proof place. Feed regularly and water freely in summer, moderately for the rest of the year. Spray the foliage occasionally.

Philodendron scandens, Sweetheart Vine, with heart-shaped dark green leaves, is the easiest of this group. Two of the non-climbing species well worth a mention are *P. bipinnatifidum*, a large plant with deeply cut leaves, and *P. wendlandii*, with elongated leaves arranged like a bird's nest.

Increase by layering, cuttings of shoot tips or stem sections.

Philodendron scandens

Opposite
Philodendron Burgundy

Phoenix roebelenii *Not so easy*

This dwarf relative of the date palm is one of the most graceful palms but it needs warmer and moister conditions than the others. Grow in a peat-based compost, water regularly and spray the foliage.

It can be raised from seeds sown in peat and sand in a warm propagator.

Phoenix roebelenii

Pilea cadierei nana

Pilea Moon Valley

Pilea (Aluminium Plant) *Easy*

Small plants which will tolerate low temperatures but prefer warm, moist shady conditions with plenty of water and good feeding. Pinch the shoot tips frequently to encourage a bushy habit.

Pilea cadierei is the species most likely to acclimatize to cooler conditions. This is called the aluminium plant for the silvery markings on the dark green leaves and there is a dwarf form which is good for terrariums. Moon Valley is an unusual variety with quilted leaves marked with brown.

Increase by stem cuttings rooted in a warm propagator.

Pteris cretica wimsettii

Platycerium (Stag's Horn Fern) *Not so easy*

A fern that is aptly named for the shape of its fronds. It is an ephiphytic plant adapted to obtaining its food from air and water and so does not need to be grown in compost. Instead it can be fastened on a basket of moss or peat or on a piece of bark or cork. Alternatively, it can be planted in a pot of peat. Ideally it should be suspended on its side as the fronds are better displayed in this way, and if grown in a pot this should be kept on its side except when the plant is watered. Frequent watering is required and is best given by plunging the piece of bark or other growing medium in water every week; weak liquid fertilizer should be added to the water occasionally. The water should be kept off the fronds and out of the centre and it is better in some warmth, good light and a humid atmosphere. It will not do well in hot, dry conditions.

Propagate from suckers.

Platycerium bifurcatum

Pteris *Easy*

Small ferns which will withstand some neglect and tolerate strong light although preferring a shady position. Water well throughout the year and feed or repot to keep them growing well.

It is the many attractive varieties of *P. cretica* which are usually offered for sale. Some of these are variegated, others have toothed or lobed fronds.

Pteris cretica albo-lineata

Rhoicissus rhomboidea

Rhoicissus rhomboidea (Grape Ivy, Natal Vine) *Easy*

A climbing plant, with glossy dark green leaves carried in threes, which supports itself with tendrils and tolerates poor growing conditions. It prefers good light and a cool, airy place. Give plenty of water in summer and feed regularly, spraying the leaves occasionally. Rhoicissus grows quickly and needs some kind of support and can look most effective if trained around a cane to make a tall pillar. Pinch the shoot tips occasionally to encourage branching.

It can be increased by cuttings which root easily in water or by layering.

Saintpaulia (African Violet) *Not so easy*

Very attractive house plants with velvety leaves and flowers which are either single or double in a range of colours – pink, violet, white, mauve, blue – and are produced almost continuously.

These are plants which do best in a fairly warm, moist atmosphere and good light but away from too much direct sunshine in summer. They are not good in draughts. Many of the new varieties, however, are more hardy and suitable for average home conditions.

Watering should be done with care as overwatering or splashing may cause the leaves to rot. This is an instance when watering from below is the better method. Plants will need frequent watering in summer, rather less in winter – always with tepid water. Feed in summer, but do not pot on too frequently, every other year is sufficient especially if you want the plants to flower. It may be difficult to get them to flower but if given a fairly sunny position and adequate warmth they should do so for most of the year.

Increase from leaves inserted in a mixture of peat and sand or in water and by division.

A selection of forms of saintpaulia

Sansevieria trifasciata laurentii

Sansevieria trifasciata Golden Hahnii

Sansevieria (Mother-in-law's Tongue) *Easy*

Familiar plants with clumps of stiff fleshy leaves, cross banded in shades of green and grey in *Sansevieria trifasciata*, and with the additional attraction of a yellow edge in *S. t. laurentii*. Older plants may produce pale green, scented flowers in summer.

They are very long suffering as they will grow in a range of conditions although preferring some sunshine and moderate heat. When potting use a clay pot if possible because plants do get rather tall and top heavy. The main cause of any problems is likely to come from overwatering. Water moderately in spring and summer but very sparingly in winter; once every few weeks is quite sufficient. Feed in summer.

There are smaller growing species *S. t. hahnii* and *S. t.* Golden Hahnii, which have low rosettes of much smaller leaves.

Propagate by suckers and leaf cuttings. The yellow edge of *S. t. laurentii* and *S. t.* Golden Hahnii cannot be reproduced by cuttings and these plants should be increased from suckers.

Schefflera actinophylla (Umbrella Tree)
Easy
This is an elegant plant, closely related to heptapleurum, which will grow to a good height indoors. The dark green leaves, composed of leaflets arranged in fans, give it a light and dainty appearance and it is ideal for display as a specimen plant.

It needs a fairly moist, warm atmosphere and good light. Water normally, allowing the soil to dry out between watering. Feed regularly in the growing season and repot annually.

Increase by seed or cuttings.

Schefflera actinophylla

Scindapsus aureus Marble Queen

Schlumbergera (Christmas Cactus) *Easy*

Formerly known as zygocactus, the Christmas cactus flowers from December to February producing its brilliantly coloured flowers from the ends of the flattened leaf-like arching stems.

Grow it in a peat-based compost, feed in summer and water all the year, restricting this a little after flowering. Try to maintain a steady temperature in winter as fluctuating temperatures along with draughts and poor watering cause buds to drop. Some warmth is necessary in winter and plants will benefit from being put out of doors in summer in a sunny, sheltered spot.

Increase by cuttings of two or three non-flowering segments which should be allowed to dry for a day or so before being inserted in peaty compost.

Scindapsus aureus *Not so easy*

This trailing plant with its glossy, bright green leaves splashed with yellow is useful for training up a moss-filled column or for trailing along a shelf. Given normal treatment it is not difficult to grow in good light and some warmth. Water freely in summer but guard against over-watering in winter. *S. aureus* Marble Queen is a variety of this with almost white leaves and it is very much more difficult to grow.

Increase by layering or cuttings rooted in peat and sand or water.

Sedum sieboldii (Ice Plant) *Easy*

An interesting small succulent creeping plant with bluish-grey leaves which is easily grown in good light and should be kept on the dry side. There is a variegated variety with cream centres to the leaves. Propagate by division or cuttings.

Spathiphyllum (White Sails) *Not so easy*

This plant is related to anthurium and requires similar conditions of warmth and humidity. It has dark green, shining, tapering leaves and creamy-white flowers (really spathes) from which it gets its common name. The flowers last well and are produced in succession over a long period.

Place in a shady position and maintain humidity by spraying the leaves or plunging pots in peat. Water well and feed in summer, keep dryer in the winter.

Divide and repot each spring.

Spathiphyllum wallisii

Stephanotis floribunda

Stephanotis floribunda (Madagascar Jasmine) *Easy*

The chief attraction of this plant is the clusters of intensely fragrant waxy white flowers produced in spring and summer.

Keep it in a light position but shade from direct sunshine in summer. Water well in spring and summer, only moderately in autumn and winter and feed in summer. Stephanotis is a good plant for the garden room where it can have a light position.

The plant produces long twining growth which can be trained to canes or a wire frame and if wound backwards and forwards as it grows flowering will be encouraged. Keep a watch for mealy bugs and scale insects. Propagate by cuttings.

Streptocarpus Constant Nymph

Streptocarpus *Easy*

Grown chiefly for the violet-blue, funnel-shaped flowers which are produced over many months. *Streptocarpus* Constant Nymph is the kind commonly available but there are also a group of new hybrids which produce solid masses of flowers in a range of blues, pinks, red and white and are specially attractive.

Grow in a peat-based compost and shade plants from strong sunshine. Keep in a cool, airy place or garden room and feed regularly in summer. A minimum temperature of 13°C. (55°F.) is necessary in winter.

Increase by leaf cuttings or division.

Tradescantia fluminensis Quicksilver

Tradescantia (Wandering Jew) *Easy*

Creeping plants which unfortunately often look rather straggly but can be most attractive and useful for growing round a container where their trailing habit and attractive colours can be appreciated.

They are not temperamental and will grow in low temperatures but prefer a light position – particularly for the variegated varieties which will turn green in poor light. Water well and feed in summer. Spray the leaves frequently as they tend to shrivel in dry air and for this reason, too, they are better in cooler temperatures in summer. To prevent plants becoming too straggly pinch the shoot tips regularly. The growth removed can be used as cuttings and will root readily in water.

Varieties are available with foliage striped in yellow, pink and white but one that is highly recommended is *Tradescantia fluminensis* Quicksilver with silver-striped leaves. If the variegated varieties produce any stems with green leaves only these should be removed as their growth is more vigorous and they will eventually take over.

Zebrina pendula *Easy*

Another trailing plant which grows happily in a range of conditions though the foliage is a better colour in good light. Water freely and feed in summer. Pinch the tips frequently to encourage branching and increase by stem cuttings.

The foliage is especially striking, the green and purple leaves have two sparkling silver bands on the upper surface and a deep purple reverse.

Zebrina pendula

Popular Florists' Plants

Azalea

Many of the flowering 'florists' plants offered for sale in shops and supermarkets throughout the year will live and flower for only a limited period in the home. A certain amount of care and a period in a greenhouse are often required if they are to flower for a second time and it is really advisable to regard them as a long-living bunch of flowers which, when compared with cut flowers, will certainly have given good value for money by the time they have to be discarded.

The general conditions required to get the best from such plants are a light, well-ventilated room, with frequent spraying to give the necessary level of humidity. The following plants are some of the ones commonly seen. The poinsettia is dealt with on page 82.

Azalea

This is the evergreen Indian azalea with its mass of single or double flowers in pink, white and red. Keep it in a draught-free position in a coolish room (13°C., 55°F.) with a steady temperature. Pick off dead flowers, spray frequently and water very freely, using soft water or rainwater if possible as this is a plant which does not like the lime in hard water.

Azaleas are the best of the florists' plants for keeping from one year to the next. After flowering, move the plant to a cooler room but do not neglect it. As soon as the danger of frost is over, stand or plunge the pot out of doors, keep well watered and feed every two weeks or so. Bring back indoors in autumn, keep in a minimum temperature of 10 to 13°C. (50 to 55°F.), and it should flower again.

Chrysanthemum

The pots of compact chrysanthemums are available in a range of subtle pinks, oranges and bronze as well as red and yellow. The plants are produced from cuttings which have been treated with a chemical to suppress growth and prevent them reaching their normal size. In addition, the plants are subjected to controlled light conditions which ensure that they flower when required rather than only in their natural season. They offer very good value for money as the flowers last for about eight weeks in a light room with little attention other than regular watering.

Once the flowers die off the plant can be grown on in the garden but as the growth suppressant loses its effect it will grow to its normal size.

Chrysanthemums

A form of *Cyclamen persicum*

Erica hyemalis

Cyclamen

Lovely plants with flowers having reflexed petals in a range of colours and dark green leaves often marked with silver. They are rather temperamental and need draught-free, light, humid conditions. When watering take care not to wet the corms and allow the compost to dry a little between watering. After flowering, the corms should be rested for the summer and given little water. Repot in late summer and grow on for a second year.

Erica (Heather)

The varieties of heather grown in pots are all South African winter-flowering kinds, and with their bell-shaped flowers in white or pink they are most welcome in winter and early spring. Keep in a warm, light room and water carefully so that the soil is never allowed to dry right out. Discard after flowering.

Sinningia speciosa

Fuchsia Blue Pearl

Fuchsia

There are many varieties of this popular plant with single or double flowers in a wide range of colours and colour combinations. They are easily raised from cuttings rooted in spring or late summer and grown on in airy conditions with shade from direct sunshine. Water freely and feed regularly during the growing season. Pinch the tops off the side shoots when these are about 4 in. long to encourage a bushy habit.

Fuchsia are not ideal house plants but are very useful for a garden room or conservatory and can be stood out of doors in summer. They should be rested in winter, given little water and kept in a cool but frost-free room.

Primula

Those offered for sale are mainly varieties of *P. obconica*, *P. malacoides*, *P. acaulis* and *P. sinensis*. Keep the plants in cool, moist, light conditions and water normally. Most should be discarded after flowering but *P. acaulis* is hardy enough to be planted in the garden.

Sinningia (Gloxinia)

These are the plants with velvety textured trumpet flowers in glorious vibrant colours. The flowers are produced from midsummer to early autumn and the plants enjoy a warm, humid atmosphere with shade from strong sun. Take care not to splash the leaves and flowers when watering. After flowering rest the tuber in a cool place, keep dry and repot in spring.

Solanum capsicastrum

This is aptly named the winter cherry for its brightly coloured berries, but it can sometimes be bought in flower in the summer and kept until the berries are produced. If obtained in summer the plant needs to be syringed with water and fed regularly. In winter it requires a light position.

It is possible to keep the plants and start new ones from cuttings taken in spring and rooted in a warm propagator, or from seeds sown in spring in a propagator.

Primula malacoides

Solanum capsicastrum